STRENGTH TRAINING
Cheat Sheet

YOUR GYM POCKET GUIDE TO
130 STRENGTH TRAINING EXERCISES

Writual
fitness

YOUR HEALTH COMES FIRST

STRENGTH TRAINING
Cheat Sheet

LET'S CONNECT

One Thing Fitness:
Join our weekly newsletter. Each week, we'll send one (yes, only one) short and to-the-point fitness email to support you on your journey. Plus, by subscribing, you'll automatically be entered into our monthly giveaways (no purchase necessary, terms and conditions apply).

Writual Fitness
writualfitness@gmail.com

  @writualfitness

Writual
fitness

OTHER PRODUCTS YOU'LL LOVE:

6 week guided workout program: Designed by a personal trainer, for beginners to follow

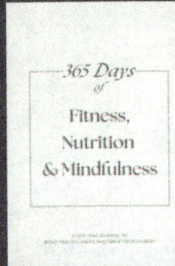

One-year wellness book: To plan and track your fitness, nutrition & mindfulness

30-Day Challenge: A new approach on building lasting habits in movement, nutrition, and mindfulness.

TABLE
OF CONTENTS

LEGS

BARBELL SQUATS

- Hold the barbell on your upper back and stand with feet shoulder-width apart
- Squat by bending your knees and pushing your hips back until thighs are parallel
- Push through your heels to stand up, squeezing your glutes at the top

- Hold the barbell on your upper back and stand with feet wider than shoulder-width, toes pointed slightly outward
- Squat by bending your knees and pushing your hips back until your thighs are parallel
- Push through your heels to stand up, squeezing your glutes at the top

BARBELL FRONT SQUATS

- Hold the barbell at shoulder level with an overhand grip and stand with feet shoulder-width apart
- Squat by bending your knees and pushing your hips back, keeping your elbows high to maintain bar position
- Push through your heels to stand up, squeezing your glutes at the top

DUMBBELL SQUATS

- Hold a dumbbell in each hand at your sides and stand with feet shoulder-width apart
- Squat by bending your knees and pushing your hips back until thighs are parallel
- Push through your heels to stand up, squeezing your glutes at the top

DUMBBELL BOX SQUATS

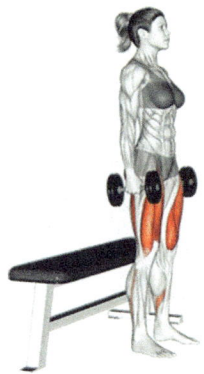 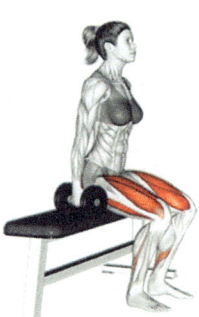

- Hold a dumbbell in each hand at your sides and stand in front of a box or bench
- Squat by bending your knees and pushing your hips back until you lightly touch the bench
- Push through your heels to stand up, squeezing your glutes at the top

- Hold a dumbbell close to your chest with both hands and stand with feet shoulder-width apart
- Squat by bending your knees and pushing your hips back, keeping the dumbbell close to your body
- Push through your heels to stand up, squeezing your glutes at the top

- Hold a dumbbell with both hands between your legs, feet in a wide stance, toes pointed out
- Lower into a squat by bending your knees, keeping your chest up and core engaged
- Push through your heels, squeezing your glutes as you return to standing

BULGARIAN SPLIT SQUATS

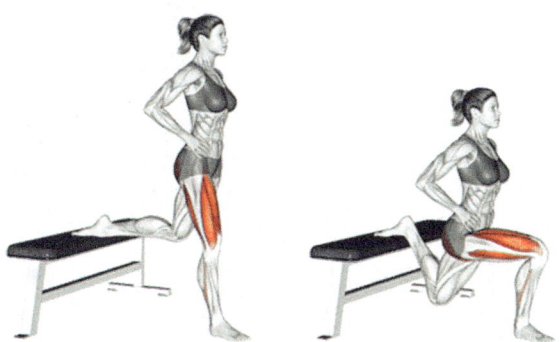

- Stand in a lunge position with one foot elevated behind you on a bench
- Lower your hips down, bending your front knee while keeping your chest upright
- Drive through your front heel, squeezing your glutes as you return to the starting position

JUMP SQUATS

- Stand with feet shoulder-width apart and lower into a squat position
- Explode upward into a jump, extending your arms overhead while pushing through your heels
- Land softly back into the squat position, keeping your knees aligned and ready for the next jump

TRX SPLIT SQUATS

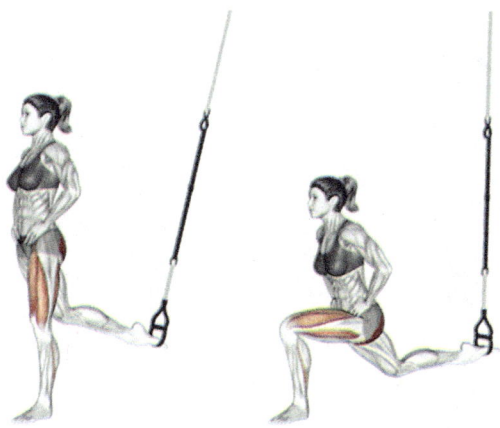

- Place one foot in the TRX handle and stand with the other foot forward in a lunge position
- Lower your hips, bending your front knee while keeping your chest upright
- Push through your front heel, squeezing your glutes as you return to the starting position

PISTOL SQUATS

LEGS

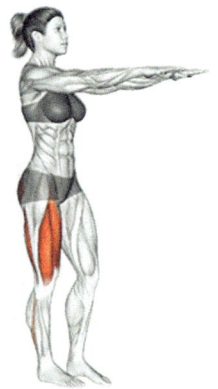

- Stand on one leg with the other leg extended in front of you, arms extended for balance
- Lower your body into a squat on the standing leg, keeping the extended leg off the ground
- Push through your heel to return to standing, squeezing your glutes at the top

- Stand with feet hip-width apart, holding a barbell or dumbbells in front of your thighs
- Hinge at your hips and bend your knees to lower the weights while keeping your back straight
- Push through your heels to stand up, squeezing your glutes at the top

ROMANIAN BARBELL DEADLIFTS

- Hold the barbell with one hand overhand and the other underhand, feet shoulder-width apart, knees slightly bent
- Hinge at your hips, lowering the barbell while keeping your back flat and glutes engaged
- Drive through your heels, squeezing your glutes as you return to standing

DUMBBELL STIFF LEG DEADLIFT

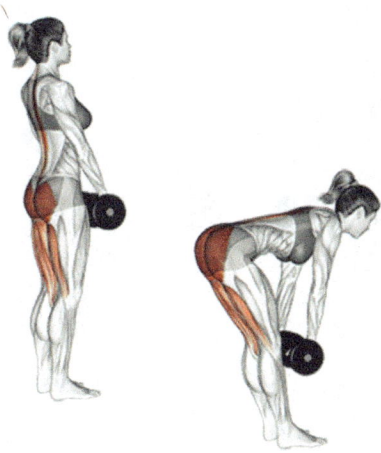

- Stand with feet hip-width apart, holding a dumbbell in each hand in front of your thighs
- Hinge at your hips while keeping your legs straight to lower the dumbbells down your legs
- Push through your heels to stand up, squeezing your glutes at the top

DUMBBELL ROMANIAN DEADLIFTS

- Hold a dumbbell in each hand, feet hip-width apart, with a slight bend in your knees
- Hinge at your hips, lowering the dumbbells while keeping your back flat and glutes engaged
- Drive through your heels, squeezing your glutes as you return to standing

SMITH MACHINE SINGLE-LEG DEADLIFT

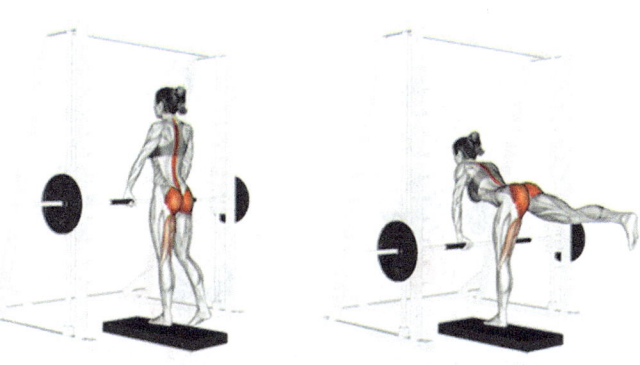

- Set the Smith machine bar to an appropriate height and stand on one leg with the other leg extended behind you
- Lower the barbell by bending at the hips while keeping your standing leg straight and back flat
- Push through your heel to return to standing, squeezing your glutes at the top

DUMBBELL LUNGES

- Stand with feet hip-width apart, holding a dumbbell in each hand at your sides
- Step forward with one leg, lowering your hips until both knees are at 90-degree angles
- Push through your front heel to return to standing and alternate legs

BARBELL LUNGES

- Hold a barbell on your upper back and stand with feet hip-width apart
- Step forward with one leg, lowering your hips until both knees are at 90-degree angles
- Push through your front heel to return to standing and alternate legs

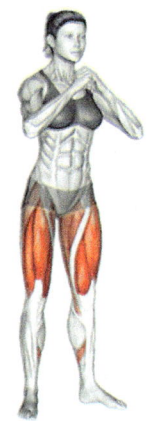

- Stand with feet shoulder-width apart, hands on your hips or in front of you for balance
- Take a big step to the side with one leg, bending that knee while keeping the other leg straight
- Push through your bent leg to return to standing and alternate sides

DUMBBELL STEP-UPS

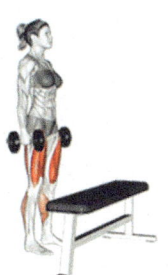 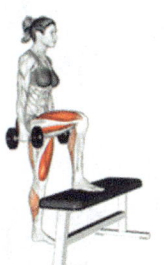 

- Stand in front of a bench or step, holding a dumbbell in each hand at your sides (or bodyweight)
- Step up onto the bench with one foot, pressing through your heel to lift your body up
- Step back down and alternate legs

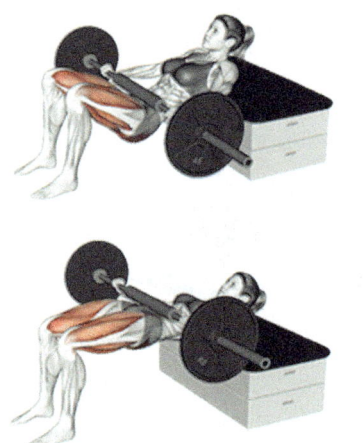

- Sit on the ground with your upper back resting on a bench and a barbell positioned over your hips
- Drive through your heels to lift your hips, squeezing your glutes at the top
- Lower your hips back down and repeat

CABLE PULL THROUGHS

- Stand facing away from a cable machine with the cable set at the lowest position and hold the handle with both hands between your legs
- Hinge at your hips and slightly bend your knees to pull the cable through your legs, keeping your back straight
- Stand up by pushing your hips forward and squeezing your glutes at the top

TRX HIP THRUSTS

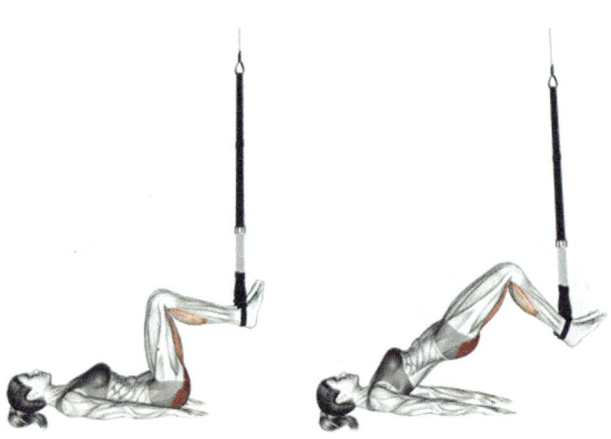

- Lie on your back with your feet in the TRX straps and your knees bent
- Press your feet into the straps, lift your hips toward the ceiling, and keep your shoulders on the ground
- Squeeze your glutes at the top and lower your hips back down without touching the ground

KETTLEBELL SWINGS

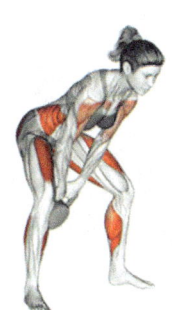
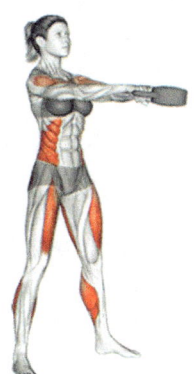

- Stand with feet shoulder-width apart, holding a kettlebell with both hands in front of you
- Hinge at your hips to lower the kettlebell between your legs while maintaining a flat back
- Thrust your hips forward to swing the kettlebell up to shoulder height, squeezing your glutes at the top

- Position your feet on the platform of the calf raise machine, with the balls of your feet on the edge
- Push through the balls of your feet to lift your heels as high as possible, then lower back down
- Repeat for the desired number of reps, focusing on the contraction in your calves

DUMBBELL CALF RAISES

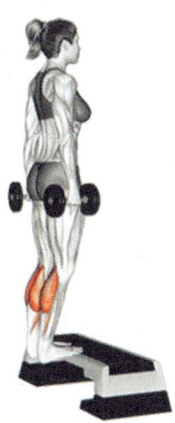
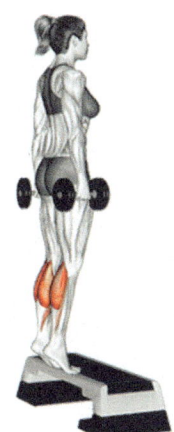

- Stand with feet hip-width apart, holding a dumbbell in each hand at your sides
- Push through the balls of your feet to lift your heels as high as possible, then lower back down
- Repeat for the desired number of reps, focusing on the contraction in your calves

- Lie on your back with a resistance band around your thighs, knees bent and feet flat on the ground
- Lift one leg off the ground, pressing through your heel on the opposite side, squeezing your glutes
- Raise your hips until your body forms a straight line from shoulders to knees, then lower back down and repeat before switching legs

STRAIGHT LEG KICKBACKS

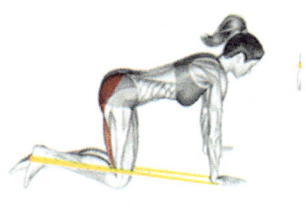

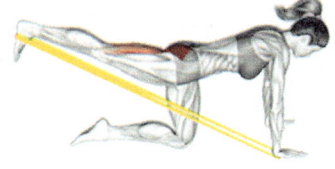

- Attach a resistance band to a low anchor point (or hand) and step back to create tension in the band
- Keeping your leg straight, kick it back while squeezing your glutes at the top of the movement
- Lower your leg back to the starting position and repeat for the desired number of reps before switching legs

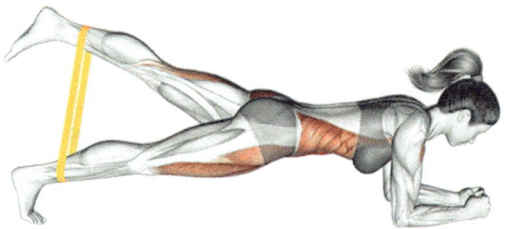

- Get into a plank position with a resistance band around your ankles and feet shoulder-width apart
- Lift one leg up, keeping it straight and squeezing your glutes at the top
- Lower your leg back down and repeat for the desired number of reps before switching legs

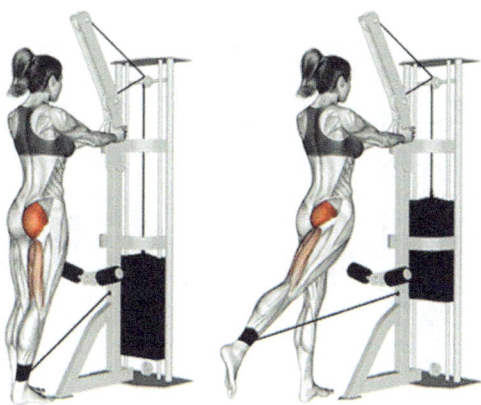

- Attach an ankle strap to a low cable pulley and secure it around your ankle
- Lift your leg straight back, keeping your knee straight and squeezing your glutes at the top
- Lower your leg back to the starting position and repeat before switching legs

CABLE HIP ADBUCTIONS

- Attach an ankle strap to a low cable pulley and secure it around your ankle, standing side-on to the machine
- Lift your leg away from your body, keeping your knee straight and squeezing your outer glutes at the top
- Lower your leg back to the starting position and repeat before switching legs

BACK

BENT-OVER DUMBBELL BENCH ROWS

- Place one knee and hand on a bench for support, with the other foot on the ground and a dumbbell in the opposite hand
- Pull the dumbbell towards your hip, keeping your elbow close to your body and squeezing your shoulder blade
- Lower the dumbbell back to the starting position and repeat before switching sides

BENT OVER DUMBBELL ROWS

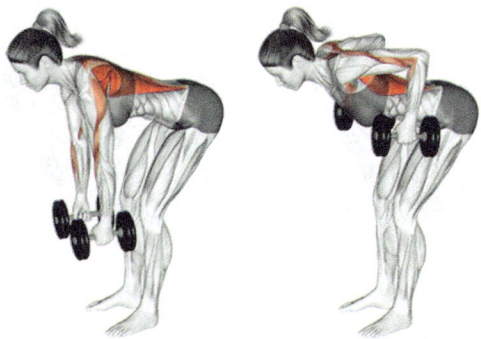

- Stand with feet hip-width apart, holding a dumbbell in each hand, and hinge at the hips
- Pull the dumbbells toward your hips, keeping your elbows close to your body and squeezing your shoulder blades
- Lower the dumbbells back to the starting position and repeat

CHEST-ASSISTED DUMBBELL ROWS

BACK

- Lay your chest against an incline bench, holding a dumbbell in each hand with arms extended down
- Pull the dumbbells towards your hips, squeezing your shoulder blades together at the top
- Lower the dumbbells back to the starting position and repeat

BANDED SEATED ROWS

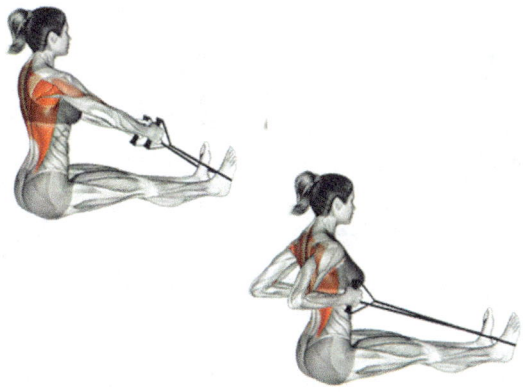

- Sit on the floor with your legs extended, wrapping a resistance band around your feet
- Hold the ends of the band with both hands and pull it towards your torso, squeezing your shoulder blades together
- Slowly return to the starting position and repeat

- Position a barbell in a landmine attachment and stand, knees bent
- Hold the end of the barbell with both hands, pulling it toward your torso while keeping your back straight
- Lower the barbell back to the starting position and repeat

- Stand with feet hip-width apart, holding a barbell with an overhand grip and bending at the hips
- Pull the barbell towards your hips, keeping your elbows close to your body and squeezing your shoulder blades
- Lower the barbell back to the starting position and repeat

DUMBBELL RENEGADE ROWS

- Get into a plank position with a dumbbell in each hand
- Row one dumbbell towards your hip while balancing on the other arm, keeping your body straight
- Lower the dumbbell back to the floor and alternate sides

CABLE SQUAT ROWS

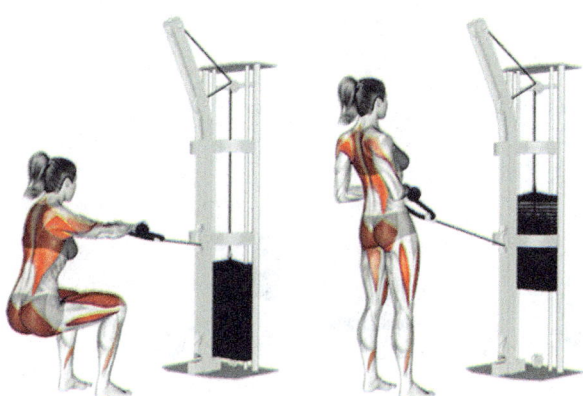

- Stand facing a cable machine with the cable set at a low position, holding the handle with both hands
- Squat down while pulling the cable towards your torso, keeping your elbows close to your body
- Stand back up while continuing to pull the cable, squeezing your shoulder blades together

SEATED CABLE ROWS

- Sit at a cable machine with feet on the platform and grab the handle with both hands
- Pull the handle towards your torso, keeping your back straight and squeezing your shoulder blades together
- Return to the starting position and repeat

CABLE FACE PULLS

BACK

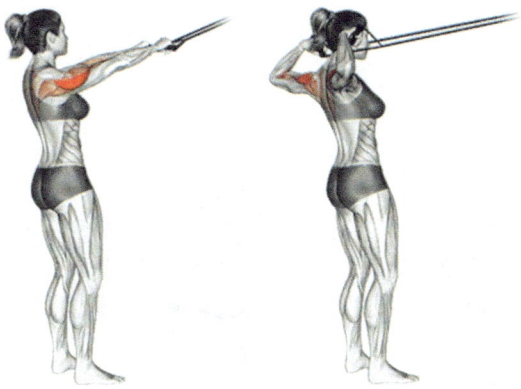

- Attach a rope to a high pulley on a cable machine and stand facing the machine
- Pull the rope towards your face, keeping your elbows high and squeezing your shoulder blades together
- Slowly return to the starting position and repeat

- Sit at a lat pulldown machine with a close grip on the bar
- Pull the bar down to your chest, keeping your elbows close to your body
- Return the bar to the starting position and repeat

SMITH MACHINE INVERTED ROWS

- Set the Smith machine bar at waist height and lie under it, gripping the bar with an underhand grip
- Pull your chest towards the bar while keeping your body straight
- Lower back down and repeat

- Hang from a pull-up bar with a wide overhand grip
- Pull your chin above the bar by engaging your back and biceps
- Lower yourself back down to the starting position and repeat

CLOSE-GRIP V-BAR PULLDOWNS

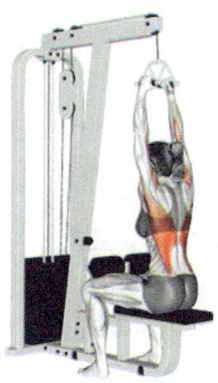 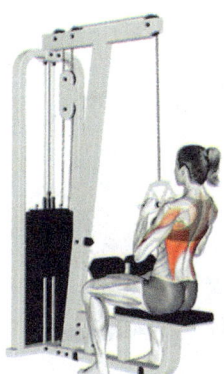

- Sit at a lat pulldown machine with a V-bar attachment and grip it with both hands close together
- Pull the V-bar down to your chest, keeping your elbows close to your body
- Slowly return to the starting position and repeat

 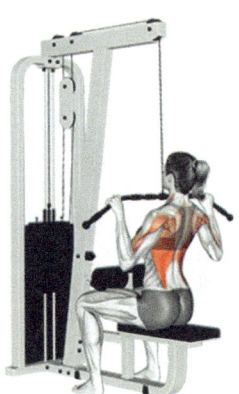

- Sit at a lat pulldown machine with a wide grip on the bar
- Pull the bar down to your chest, focusing on engaging your back muscles
- Return the bar to the starting position and repeat

ASSISTED CLOSE-GRIP CHIN UPS

BACK

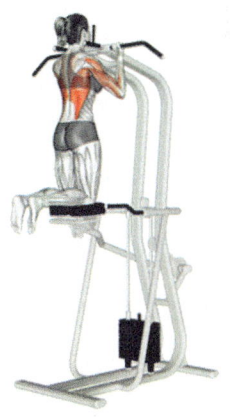
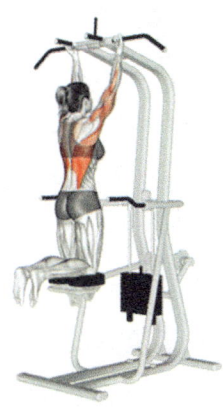

- Grab the chin-up bar with an underhand, close grip, and step onto the assistance platform or band
- Pull yourself up until your chin is above the bar, squeezing your biceps and back
- Lower yourself back down in a controlled motion, fully extending your arms

- Hold the TRX handles with your arms extended, palms facing each other, and lean back with your body straight
- Pull your chest towards the handles, squeezing your shoulder blades together
- Lower yourself back to the starting position with control

STRAIGHT ARM PULLDOWNS

BACK

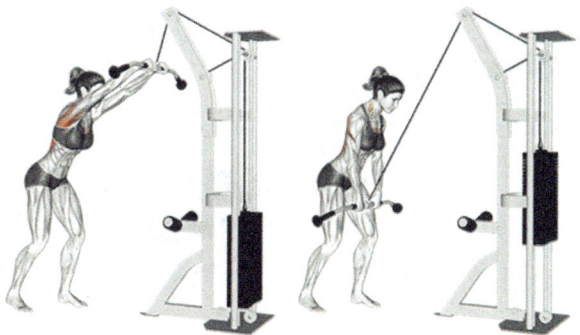

- Stand in front of a cable machine with a straight bar attachment at the highest setting
- Grab the bar with both hands and pull it down towards your thighs while keeping your arms straight
- Slowly return to the starting position and repeat

DUMBBELL PULLOVERS

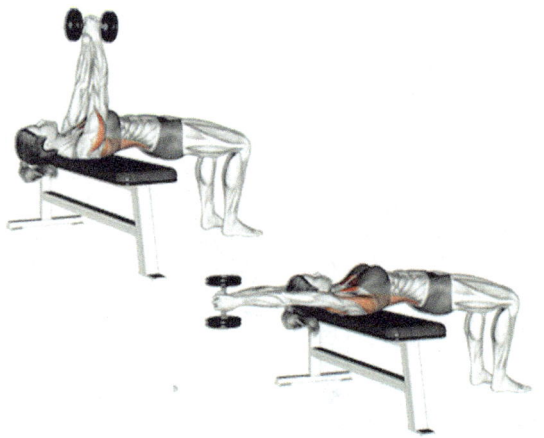

- Lie on a bench with your upper back supported and hold a dumbbell with both hands above your chest
- Lower the dumbbell back over your head while keeping your arms slightly bent
- Pull the dumbbell back to the starting position, engaging your chest and lats

CHEST

BARBELL FLAT BENCH PRESS

- Lie on a flat bench with your feet flat on the ground and grip the barbell with hands slightly wider than shoulder-width
- Lower the barbell to your chest, keeping your elbows at a 45-degree angle
- Push the barbell back up to the starting position while engaging your chest muscles

INCLINE BARBELL BENCH PRESS

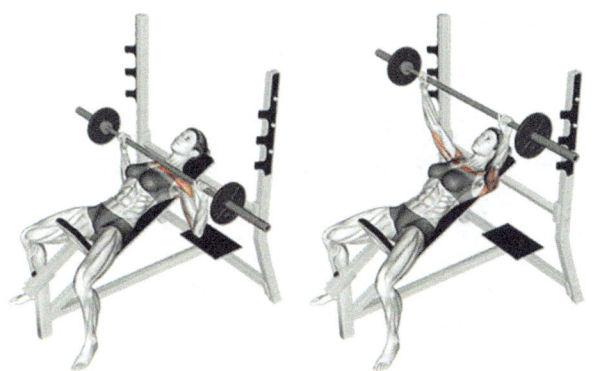

- Set the bench to a 30-45 degree incline and lie back, gripping the barbell with hands slightly wider than shoulder-width
- Lower the barbell to your upper chest, keeping your elbows at a 45-degree angle
- Push the barbell back up to the starting position while engaging your upper chest

DECLINE BARBELL BENCH PRESS

- Set the bench to a decline and lie back, gripping the barbell with hands slightly wider than shoulder-width
- Lower the barbell to your lower chest, keeping your elbows at a 45-degree angle
- Push the barbell back up to the starting position while engaging your lower chest

FLAT BENCH DUMBBELL PRESS

- Lie on a flat bench with a dumbbell in each hand, arms extended above your chest
- Lower the dumbbells to your chest, keeping your elbows at a 45-degree angle
- Press the dumbbells back up to the starting position while engaging your chest

DECLINE DUMBBELL BENCH PRESS

- Set the bench to a decline and lie back, holding a dumbbell in each hand above your chest
- Lower the dumbbells to your lower chest, keeping your elbows at a 45-degree angle
- Press the dumbbells back up to the starting position while engaging your lower chest

INCLINE DUMBBELL PRESS

- Set the bench to a 30-45 degree incline and lie back, holding a dumbbell in each hand above your chest
- Lower the dumbbells to your upper chest, keeping your elbows at a 45-degree angle
- Press the dumbbells back up to the starting position while engaging your upper chest

INCLINE DUMBBELL CHEST FLYS

- Set the bench to a 30-45 degree incline and lie back with a dumbbell in each hand, arms extended above your chest
- Lower the dumbbells out to the sides, keeping a slight bend in your elbows
- Bring the dumbbells back together above your chest, squeezing your chest muscles

CABLE LOW FLYS

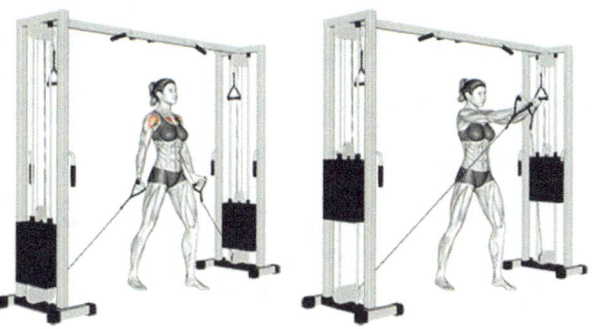

- Stand in the center of a cable machine with the pulleys set low and grab the handles
- With a slight bend in your elbows, bring the handles up and together in front of your chest
- Return to the starting position, keeping tension in the cables

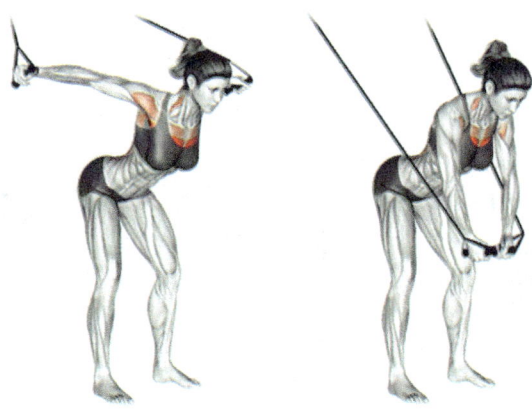

- Stand in the center of a cable machine with the pulleys set high and grab the handles
- With a slight bend in your elbows, bring the handles down and together in front of your chest
- Return to the starting position, keeping tension in the cables

DUMBBELL CHEST FLYS

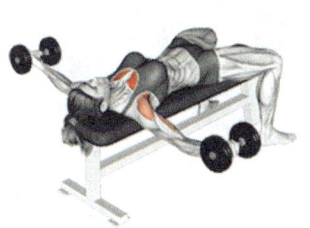 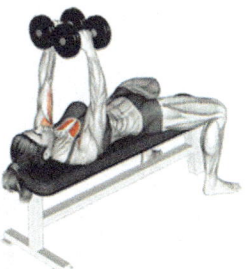

- Lie on a flat bench with a dumbbell in each hand, arms extended above your chest
- Lower the dumbbells out to the sides, keeping a slight bend in your elbows
- Bring the dumbbells back together above your chest, squeezing your chest muscles

INCLINE CABLE CHEST FLYS

- Set the pulleys on a cable machine to a low position and lie back on an incline bench
- Grab the handles with arms extended above your chest and a slight bend in your elbows
- Lower the handles out to the sides in a wide arc, then bring them back together above your chest, squeezing your chest muscles

DUMBBELL PUSH-UPS

- Hold a dumbbell in each hand while in a push-up position
- Lower your body towards the ground, keeping your elbows close to your sides
- Push back up to the starting position, engaging your chest and triceps

TRX PUSH-UPS

- Secure the TRX straps to your feet and get into a push-up position with your hands on the ground
- Lower your body towards the ground, keeping your elbows close to your sides
- Push back up to the starting position, engaging your chest and triceps

DECLINE STABILITY BALL PUSH-UPS

CHEST

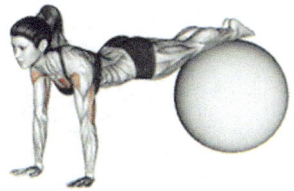

- Place your feet on a stability ball and hands on the ground in a push-up position
- Lower your body towards the ground, keeping your elbows close to your sides
- Push back up to the starting position, engaging your chest and triceps

CHEST DIPS

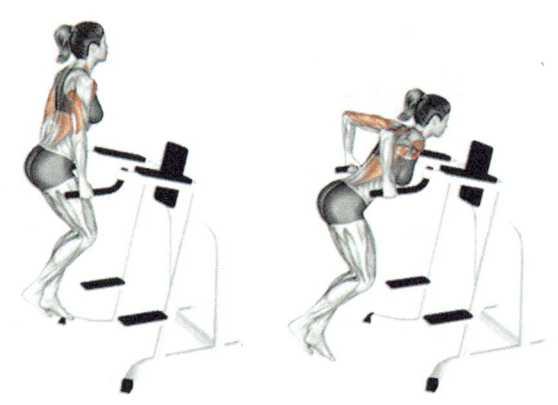

- Use dip bars to support your body weight, keeping your arms straight
- Leaning forward, lower your body by bending your elbows until your upper arms are parallel to the ground
- Push back up to the starting position, engaging your chest and triceps

TRX CHEST FLYS

- Hold the TRX straps with both hands and lean back, keeping your body straight
- Lower your arms out to the sides in a wide arc while keeping a slight bend in your elbows
- Bring your arms back together in front of your chest, squeezing your chest muscles

- Stand facing away from the TRX anchor point and hold the straps at shoulder height
- Lean forward, bending your elbows, and lower your body towards the ground
- Push back to the starting position, engaging your chest and triceps

SHOULDERS

- Stand with feet shoulder-width apart, holding a dumbbell in each hand at shoulder height
- Press the dumbbells overhead until your arms are fully extended
- Lower the dumbbells back to shoulder height and repeat

SEATED OVERHEAD DUMBBELL PRESSES

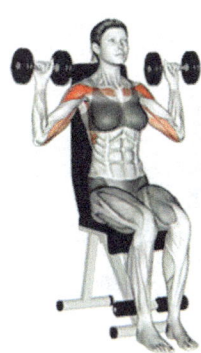

- Sit on a bench with back support, holding a dumbbell in each hand at shoulder height
- Press the dumbbells overhead until your arms are fully extended
- Lower the dumbbells back to shoulder height and repeat

- Sit on a bench with back support, holding a dumbbell in each hand at shoulder height, palms facing you
- As you press the dumbbells overhead, rotate your palms to face forward
- Lower the dumbbells back to the starting position, rotating your palms back towards you

SEATED LATERAL RAISES

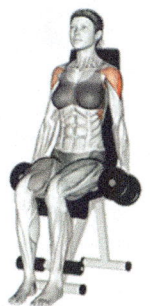 

- Sit on a bench with a dumbbell in each hand at your sides
- Raise the dumbbells out to the sides until they reach shoulder height, keeping a slight bend in your elbows
- Lower the dumbbells back to the starting position and repeat

DUMBBELL FRONT RAISES

SHOULDERS

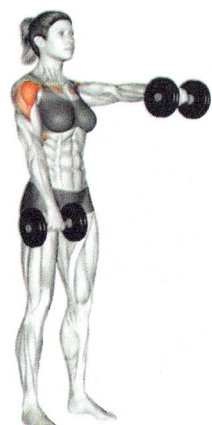

- Stand with feet shoulder-width apart, holding a dumbbell in one hand at your thigh
- Raise the dumbbell in front of you to shoulder height, keeping your arm straight
- Lower the dumbbell back to the starting position and repeat before switching sides

DUMBBELL LATERAL RAISES

SHOULDERS

 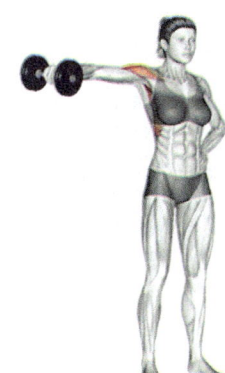

- Stand with feet shoulder-width apart, holding a dumbbell in one hand at your side
- Raise the dumbbell out to the side until it reaches shoulder height, keeping a slight bend in your elbow
- Lower the dumbbell back to the starting position and repeat before switching sides

BENT-OVER DUMBBELL RAISES

- Stand with feet shoulder-width apart and bend at the hips, holding a dumbbell in each hand with palms facing each other
- Raise the dumbbells out to the sides, squeezing your shoulder blades together at the top
- Lower the dumbbells back to the starting position and repeat

INCLINE REVERSE FLYS

- Lie face down on an incline bench with a dumbbell in each hand, arms hanging straight down
- Raise the dumbbells out to the sides, keeping a slight bend in your elbows
- Lower the dumbbells back to the starting position and repeat

CABLE LATERAL RAISES

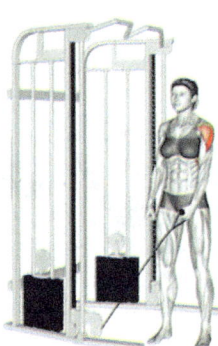 

- Stand next to a cable machine, holding the handle in one hand with the pulley set to the lowest position
- Raise the handle out to the side until your arm reaches shoulder height, keeping a slight bend in your elbow
- Lower the handle back to the starting position and repeat before switching sides

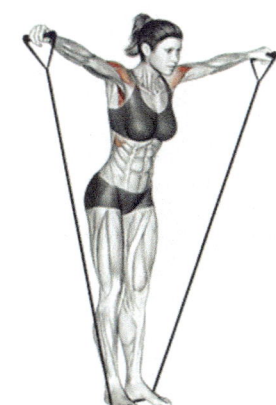

- Stand with feet shoulder-width apart, holding a resistance band with both hands at your sides
- Step on the band to anchor it, then raise your arms out to the sides until they reach shoulder height
- Lower your arms back to the starting position and repeat

BARBELL SHRUGS

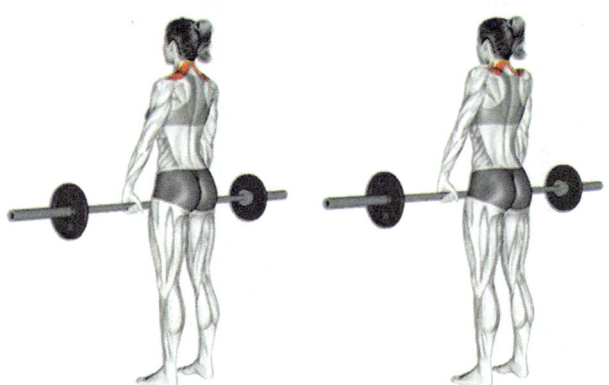

- Stand with feet shoulder-width apart, holding a barbell in front of your thighs with both hands
- Raise your shoulders towards your ears, squeezing your traps at the top
- Lower your shoulders back down and repeat

BARBELL UPRIGHT ROWS

- Stand with feet shoulder-width apart, holding a barbell with both hands in front of your thighs
- Pull the barbell up towards your chin, keeping it close to your body and your elbows higher than your wrists
- Lower the barbell back to the starting position and repeat

DUMBBELL SHRUGS

SHOULDERS

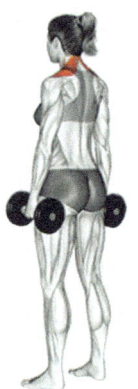

- Stand with feet shoulder-width apart, holding a dumbbell in each hand at your sides
- Raise your shoulders towards your ears, squeezing your traps at the top
- Lower your shoulders back down and repeat

DUMBBELL LYING EXTERNAL ROTATIONS

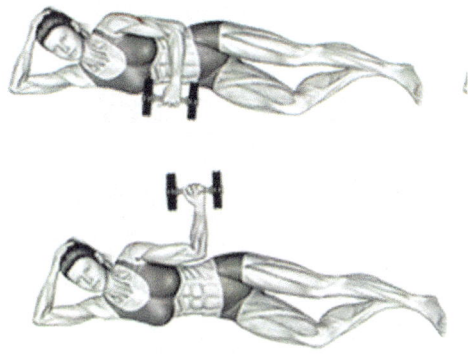

- Lie on your side with your bottom arm supporting your head and the top hand holding a light dumbbell.
- Bend your top elbow at 90 degrees, keeping it against your side.
- Rotate your arm to lift the dumbbell upward, then lower with control.

CABLE INTERNAL ROTATIONS

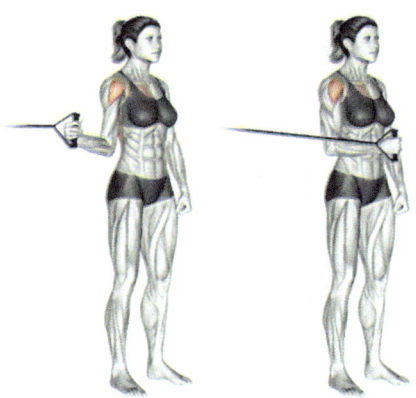

- Stand next to a cable machine with the pulley set at elbow height, holding the handle in one hand
- Keep your elbow close to your body and rotate your arm inward, pulling the handle across your torso
- Return to the starting position and repeat before switching sides

EXTERNAL CABLE ROTATIONS

SHOULDERS

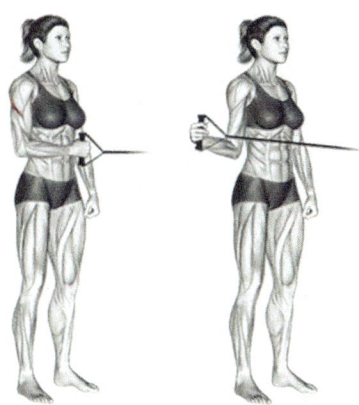

- Stand next to a cable machine with the pulley set at elbow height, holding the handle with one hand
- Keeping your elbow close to your body, rotate your arm outward, squeezing your shoulder muscles
- Return to the starting position and repeat before switching sides

TRICEPS

BARBELL SKULL CRUSHERS

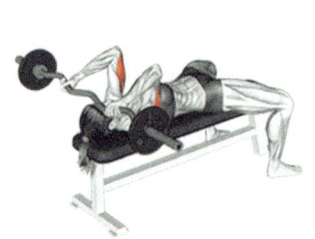 

- Lie on a flat bench, holding a barbell with arms extended above your chest
- Lower the barbell towards your forehead by bending your elbows, keeping your upper arms stationary
- Extend your arms back to the starting position, engaging your triceps

DUMBBELL LYING EXTENSIONS

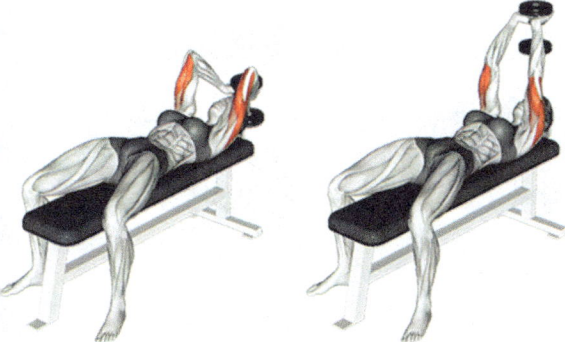

- Lie on a flat bench, holding a dumbbell in each hand with arms extended above your chest
- Lower the dumbbells towards your forehead by bending your elbows, keeping your upper arms stationary
- Extend your arms back to the starting position, engaging your triceps

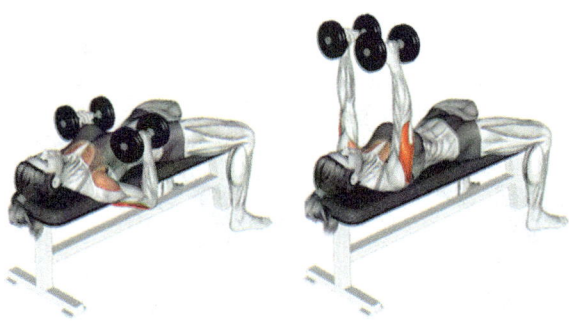

- Lie on a flat bench, holding two dumbbells together above your chest with palms facing each other
- Lower the dumbbells towards your chest while keeping them close together
- Press the dumbbells back up to the starting position, engaging your triceps

SUPINATED TRICEP EXTENSIONS

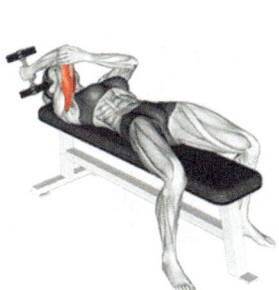

- Lie on a flat bench, holding a dumbbell in one hand with your palm facing up
- Lower the dumbbell behind your head by bending your elbow, keeping your upper arm stationary
- Extend your arm back to the starting position, engaging your triceps before switching sides

SEATED DUMBELL TRICEP EXTENSIONS

- Sit on a bench, holding a dumbbell with both hands above your head, arms fully extended
- Lower the dumbbell behind your head by bending your elbows, keeping your upper arms stationary
- Extend your arms back to the starting position, engaging your triceps

DUMBBELL KICKBACKS

- Kneel on a bench with one knee and one hand for support, holding a dumbbell in the opposite hand
- Keep your upper arm parallel to the ground and extend your arm back while keeping your elbow close to your body
- Lower the dumbbell back to the starting position and repeat before switching sides

CABLE KICKBACKS

TRICEPS

- Stand facing a cable machine with the pulley set low, holding the handle in one hand
- Bend at the hips and keep your back flat, then extend your arm back while keeping your elbow close to your body
- Lower the handle back to the starting position and repeat before switching sides

CABLE PUSHDOWNS

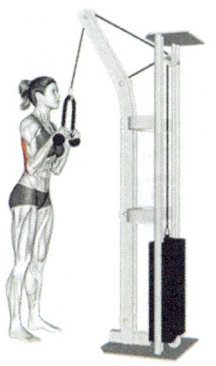 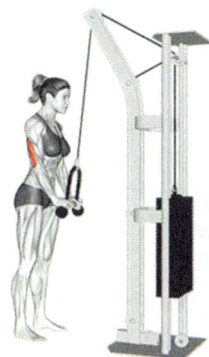

- Stand facing a cable machine with the pulley set high, holding the handle with both hands
- Keep your elbows close to your body and push the handle down until your arms are fully extended
- Return to the starting position and repeat

CABLE OVERHEAD EXTENSIONS

 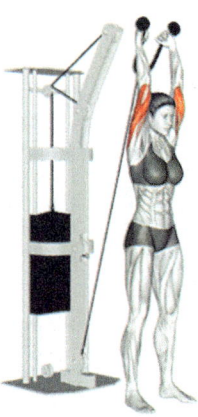

- Stand facing away from a cable machine with the pulley set at the lowest position, holding the handle with both hands
- Lift the handle above your head, keeping your elbows close to your ears
- Lower the handle behind your head by bending your elbows, then extend your arms back to the starting position, engaging your triceps

- Attach a resistance band to a high anchor point and grasp the band with both hands, elbows bent and close to your head
- Extend your arms downwards, fully straightening your elbows while keeping your upper arms stationary
- Return to the starting position with control, keeping tension in the band throughout the movement

CLOSE-GRIP BARBELL BENCH PRESS

TRICEPS

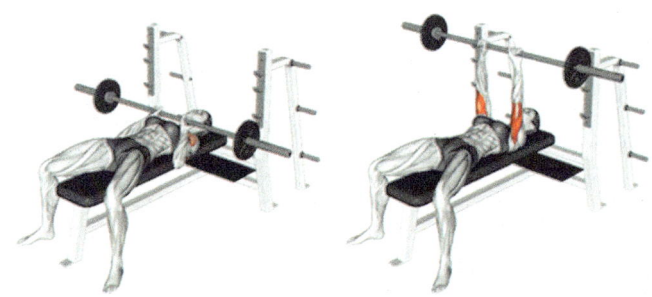

- Lie on a flat bench, holding a barbell with hands closer than shoulder-width apart
- Lower the barbell to your chest while keeping your elbows close to your body
- Press the barbell back up to the starting position, engaging your triceps

CLOSE GRIP PUSH-UPS

- Get into a push-up position with hands placed closer than shoulder-width apart
- Lower your body towards the ground, keeping your elbows close to your sides
- Push back up to the starting position, engaging your triceps

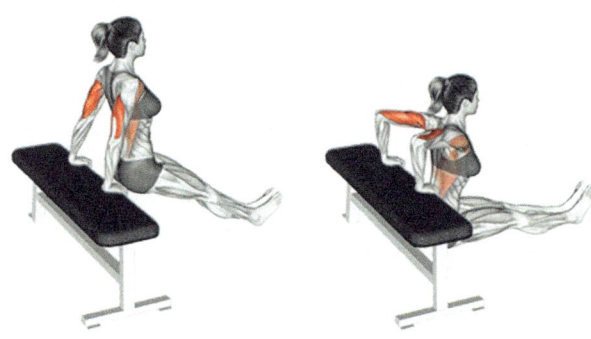

- Sit on the edge of a bench with hands next to your thighs, fingers facing forward
- Lower your body towards the ground by bending your elbows, keeping your back close to the bench
- Push back up to the starting position, engaging your triceps

ASSISTED MACHINE DIPS

- Position yourself on an assisted dip machine, adjusting the weight for support
- Lower your body by bending your elbows, keeping your upper arms close to your sides
- Push back up to the starting position, engaging your triceps

BICEPS

BARBELL CURLS

- Stand with feet shoulder-width apart, holding a barbell with an underhand grip
- Curl the barbell up towards your chest, keeping your elbows close to your sides
- Lower the barbell back to the starting position and repeat

SEATED BICEP CURLS

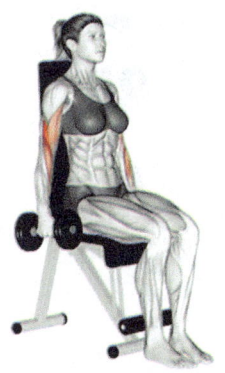 

- Sit on a bench with a dumbbell in each hand, arms fully extended at your sides
- Curl the dumbbells up towards your shoulders while keeping your elbows stationary
- Lower the dumbbells back to the starting position and repeat

DUMMBELL CURLS

BICEPS

- Stand with feet shoulder-width apart, holding a dumbbell in one hand at your side
- Curl the dumbbell up towards your shoulder, keeping your elbow close to your side
- Lower the dumbbell back to the starting position and repeat before switching sides

BARBELL PREACHER CURLS

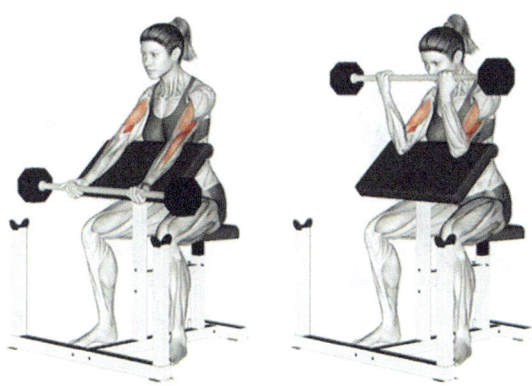

- Sit on a preacher bench, holding a barbell with an underhand grip, arms extended down
- Curl the barbell towards your shoulders, keeping your upper arms against the bench
- Lower the barbell back to the starting position and repeat

INCLINE BICEP CURLS

- Sit on an incline bench with a dumbbell in each hand, arms hanging straight down
- Curl the dumbbells up towards your shoulders while keeping your elbows stationary
- Lower the dumbbells back to the starting position and repeat

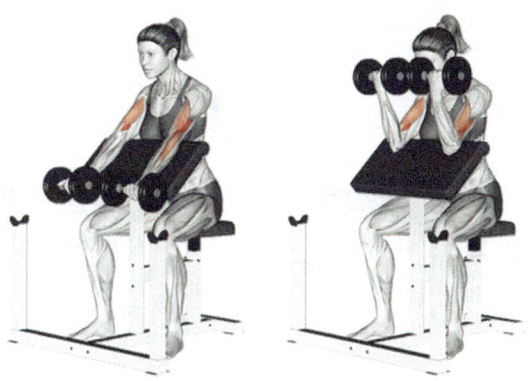

- Sit on a preacher bench with a dumbbell in each hand, arms extended down
- Curl the dumbbells towards your shoulders, keeping your upper arms against the bench
- Lower the dumbbells back to the starting position and repeat

CONCENTRATION CURLS

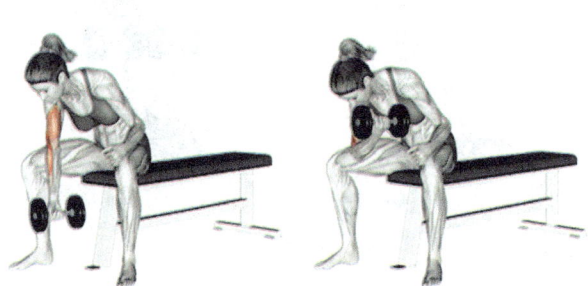

- Sit on a bench with your legs apart, resting your elbow against the inside of your thigh
- Curl the dumbbell towards your shoulder, focusing on squeezing your bicep at the top
- Lower the dumbbell back to the starting position and repeat before switching sides

HAMMER CURLS

BICEPS

- Stand with feet shoulder-width apart, holding a dumbbell in each hand with palms facing each other
- Curl the dumbbells up towards your shoulders, keeping your elbows close to your sides
- Lower the dumbbells back to the starting position and repeat

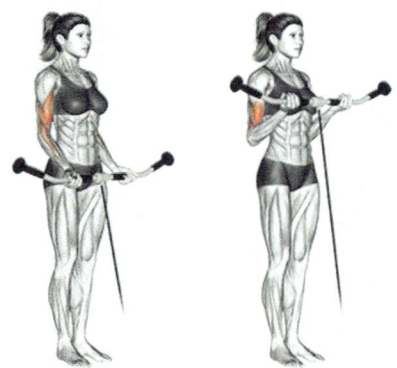

- Stand facing a cable machine with the pulley set low, holding the handle with an underhand grip
- Curl the handle towards your shoulders, keeping your elbows stationary
- Lower the handle back to the starting position and repeat

CORE

BIRD DOGS

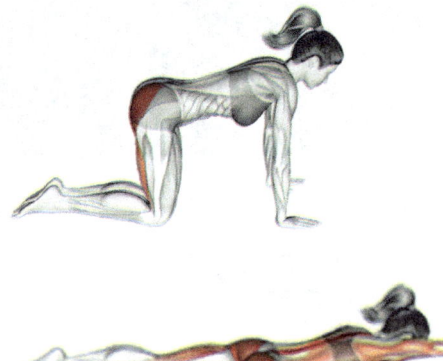

- Start on all fours with hands under shoulders and knees under hips
- Extend one arm forward and the opposite leg back, keeping your body stable
- Return to the starting position and switch sides

DEAD BUGS

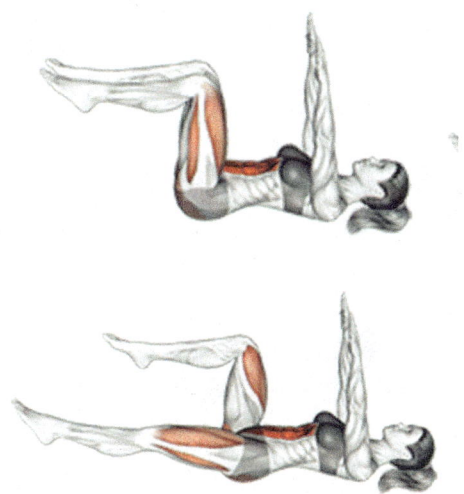

- Lie on your back with arms extended towards the ceiling and knees bent at 90 degrees
- Slowly lower your right arm and left leg towards the floor while keeping your back flat
- Return to the starting position and switch sides

SUPERMANS

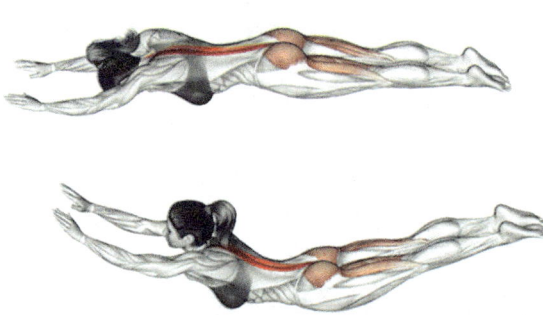

- Lie face down with arms extended in front of you
- Simultaneously lift your arms, chest, and legs off the ground while engaging your back
- Lower back to the starting position and repeat

MOUNTAIN CLIMBERS

CORE

- Start in a push-up position with your hands under your shoulders
- Quickly bring one knee towards your chest, then switch legs in a running motion
- Continue alternating legs at a steady pace

FRONT PLANK

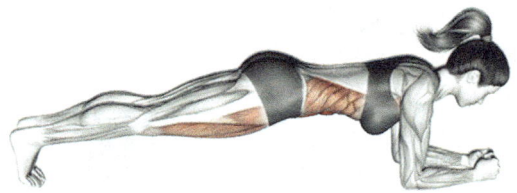

- Lie face down, then lift your body off the ground, supporting yourself on your forearms and toes
- Keep your body in a straight line from head to heels, engaging your core
- Hold this position for the desired time

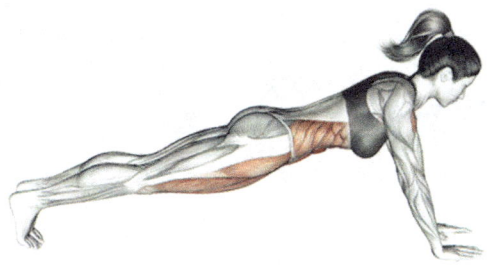

- Lie face down, then lift your body off the ground, supporting yourself on your hands and toes
- Keep your body in a straight line from head to heels, engaging your core
- Hold this position for the desired time

TRX SUSPENDED JACKKNIFE

- Set TRX straps to mid-calf length and place your feet in the foot cradles
- Start in a plank position, then pull your knees towards your chest, engaging your core
- Extend your legs back to the starting position and repeat

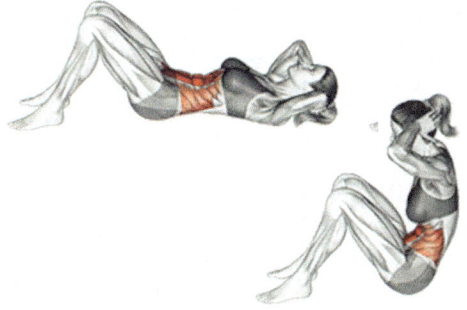

- Lie on your back with knees bent and feet flat on the ground
- Curl your torso up until you are at a 3/4 angle, engaging your core
- Lower back down to the starting position and repeat

- Lie on your back with hands behind your head and legs lifted at a 90-degree angle
- Bring one knee towards your chest while extending the opposite leg, twisting your torso to bring your elbow towards the knee
- Alternate sides in a pedaling motion

- Lie flat on your back with arms extended above your head and legs straight
- Simultaneously lift your arms and legs towards each other, forming a V shape with your body
- Lower back to the starting position and repeat

STABILITY BALL CRUNCHES

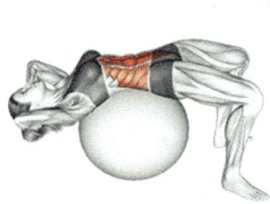
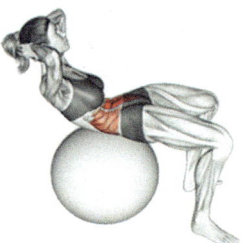

- Sit on a stability ball and walk your feet forward until your lower back is supported by the ball
- Place your hands behind your head, keeping your elbows wide
- Curl your torso up towards your knees, engaging your core, then lower back to the starting position and repeat

CABLE CRUNCHES

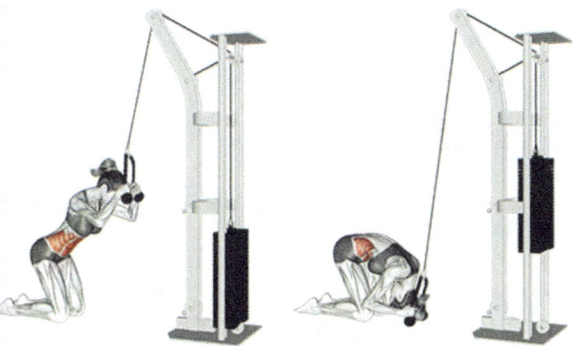

- Kneel in front of a cable machine with the pulley set high, holding the rope handle with both hands
- Pull the cable down towards your knees, crunching your torso forward
- Return to the starting position and repeat

- Kneel on the floor with an ab wheel in front of you
- Roll the wheel forward while keeping your back straight and engaging your core
- Roll back to the starting position and repeat

CAPTAIN'S CHAIR STRAIGHT LEG RAISE

CORE

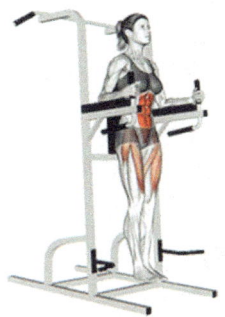 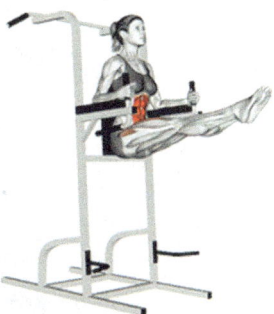

- Stand on the captain's chair with your back against the support and arms resting on the side pads
- Engage your core and lift your legs straight up until they are parallel to the ground
- Lower your legs back to the starting position without swinging and repeat

DECLINE REVERSE CRUNCH

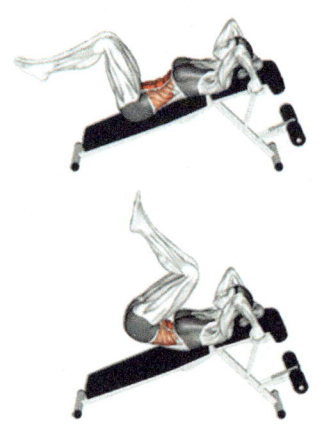

- Lie on a decline bench with your legs hanging off the end
- Curl your knees towards your chest while lifting your hips off the bench
- Lower back to the starting position and repeat

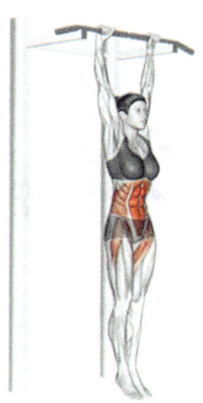

- Hang from a pull-up bar with your arms extended and legs bent at the knees
- Engage your core and raise your knees towards your chest, keeping your back straight
- Lower your legs back to the starting position with control and repeat

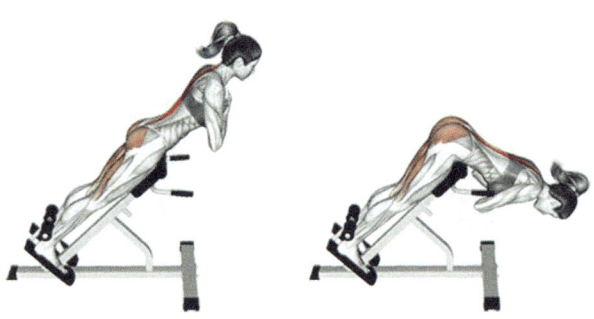

- Lie face down on a hyperextension bench with your hips supported
- Lower your upper body towards the ground, then raise it back up until your body is in a straight line
- Lower back to the starting position and repeat

LYING SCISSOR KICKS

- Lie on your back with legs extended and hands under your hips
- Lift your legs slightly off the ground and alternate crossing them over each other
- Continue alternating while engaging your core

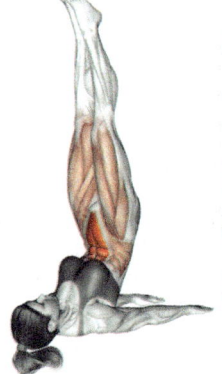

- Lie on your back with legs straight and hands under your hips
- Lift your legs towards the ceiling while keeping them straight
- Lower back down to just above the ground and repeat

DUMBBELL SIDE BEND

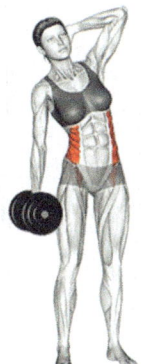 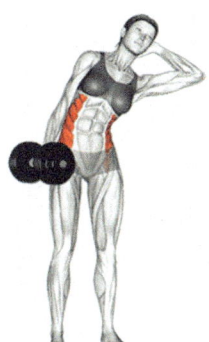

- Stand with feet shoulder-width apart, holding a dumbbell in one hand at your side
- Bend to the side, lowering the dumbbell towards your knee while keeping your other arm raised
- Return to the starting position and repeat before switching sides

KNEELING CABLE TWIST

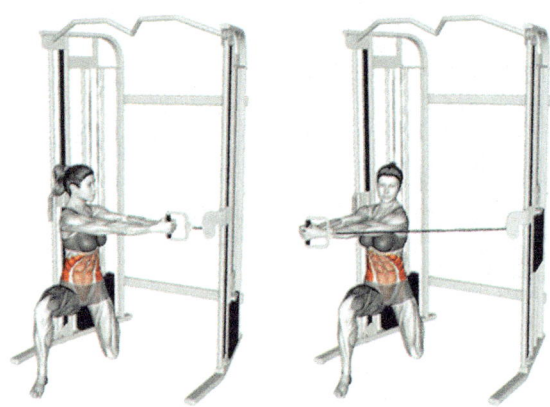

- Kneel in front of a cable machine with the pulley set to a low position, holding the handle with both hands
- Twist your torso away from the machine, engaging your core throughout
- Return to the starting position and repeat before switching sides

STANDING CABLE TWIST

CORE

- Stand facing away from a cable machine with the pulley set at shoulder height, holding the handle with both hands
- Rotate your torso away from the machine, engaging your core throughout
- Return to the starting position and repeat before switching sides

STABILITY BALL SIDE SIDE CRUNCHES

- Lie on your side on a stability ball, with your feet planted on the ground for balance
- Place one hand behind your head and the other hand on your hip
- Engage your core and bend to the side, lowering your torso towards the ground, then return to the starting position and repeat before switching sides

SIDE PLANK

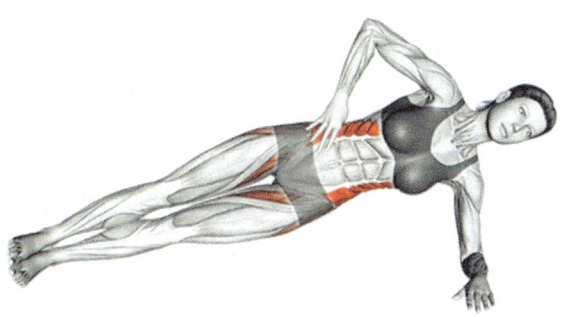

- Lie on your side with your legs stacked, propping your upper body up on your elbow
- Lift your hips off the ground, forming a straight line from head to heels
- Hold this position for the desired time before switching sides

Made in the USA
Coppell, TX
28 February 2025

46514315R00085